CENGAGE Learning

Poetry for Students, Volume 35

Project Editor: Sara Constantakis Rights Acquisition and Management: Margaret Chamberlain-Gaston, Kelly Quin, Aja Perales, Robyn Young Composition: Evi Abou-El-Seoud Manufacturing: Drew Kalasky

Imaging: John Watkins

Product Design: Pamela A. E. Galbreath, Jennifer Wahi Content Conversion: Katrina Coach Product Manager: Meggin Condino of the publisher.

Since this page cannot legibly accommodate all copyright notices, the acknowledgments constitute an extension of the copyright notice.

For product information and technology assistance, contact us at
Gale Customer Support, 1-800-877-4253.
For permission to use material from this text or product,
submit all requests online at
www.cengage.com/permissions.
Further permissions questions can be emailed to
permissionrequest@cengage.com While every effort has been made to ensure the reliability of the information presented in this publication, Gale, a part of Cengage Learning, does not guarantee the accuracy of the data contained herein. Gale accepts no payment for listing; and inclusion in the publication of any organization, agency, institution, publication, service, or individual does not imply endorsement of the editors or publisher. Errors brought to the attention of the publisher and verified to the satisfaction of the publisher will be corrected in future editions.

Gale
27500 Drake Rd.
Farmington Hills, MI, 48331-3535

ISBN-13: 978-1-4144-4183-2
ISBN-10: 1-4144-4183-5
ISSN 1094-7019

This title is also available as an e-book.

ISBN-13: 978-1-4144-4956-2
ISBN-10: 1-4144-4956-9
Contact your Gale, a part of Cengage Learning sales
representative for ordering information.

Printed in the United States of America
1 2 3 4 5 6 7 14 13 12 11 10

Childe Harold's Pilgrimage

LORD BYRON

1818

INTRODUCTION

The seven stanzas beginning with "There is a pleasure in the pathless woods," are stanzas CLXXVIII to CLXXXIV (178-184) of Canto IV of *Childe Harold's Pilgrimage*, published in 1818 by Lord Byron, one of the greatest of the English Romantic poets. The last six of these stanzas are also known as the apostrophe to the ocean, since they are directly addressed to the ocean.

    Childe Harold's Pilgrimage is a long, semiautobiographical poem in which Byron records his impressions of places he visited during several tours of Europe, the first of which took place in 1811. Childe is the medieval title for a young man who was soon to become a knight.

The first two cantos of the poem were published in 1812, and Canto III followed in 1816. In 1817, Byron visited Venice and Rome, and his reflections on what he saw there form the basis of Canto IV. In May 1817, Byron went to the top of the Alban Mount, near Rome, from which he was able to gaze out at the Mediterranean Sea, and this experience inspired the stanzas addressed to the ocean in *Childe Harold's Pilgrimage*. These stanzas are examples of the Spenserian stanzas that Byron uses throughout the poem. They show Byron's love of nature and also reveal his meditations on the passing of time and the transience of human endeavors.

AUTHOR BIOGRAPHY

George Gordon, Lord Byron, was born into an aristocratic family in London, England, on January 22, 1788. His mother was a Scot, Catherine Gordon, and his father was Captain John ("Mad Jack") Byron. The captain had wasted Catherine's fortune before Byron was born, and his mother took the child to Aberdeen, Scotland, while John Byron lived a dissolute life in Paris until his death in 1791. Byron became heir to the family title at the age of six, and when he was made Lord Byron in 1798, he was taken by his mother to live at Newstead Abbey, the Byrons' ancestral estate, in England.

Byron was schooled in London and at Trinity College, Cambridge, although he only spent a term there before returning to London, where he accumulated debts. In 1809, Byron traveled to Europe with his friend John Cam Hobhouse. They visited Portugal, Spain, Gibraltar, Malta, Greece, Albania, and Turkey. He returned in July 1811 and published *Childe Harold's Pilgrimage*, an account in verse of his travels and his reflections. The poem immediately made him famous, and he started to move in aristocratic society in London, gaining the interest and admiration of many women. These included Lady Caroline Lamb, with whom Byron had an affair, but eventually he rejected her. Instead, he fell in love with his half-sister Augusta Leigh, but he eventually married Annabella Milbanke in 1815. The marriage was unsuccessful, and they separated a year later. Now the subject of much scandal, Byron left England permanently in April 1816. By that time he had become a renowned poet not only for *Childe Harold's Pilgrimage* but also for a series of verse narratives known as Oriental tales. These were *The Giaour* (1813), *The Bride of Abydos* (1813), *The Corsair* (1814), and *Lara* (1814).

Byron spent the summer of 1816 in Switzerland with another English poet, Percy Bysshe Shelley, and his circle. In that year, Byron published Canto III of *Childe Harold* as well as *The Prisoner of Chillon*. In 1817, Byron lived in Venice, where he had an affair with the married Marianna Segati, and visited Florence and Rome. He also published his verse drama *Manfred* (1817). The following year he published Canto IV of *Childe Harold*, in which the apostrophe to the ocean appears.

In 1819, the first two cantos of *Don Juan*, Byron's comic masterpiece, were published. This was also the year in which Byron began his liaison with another married woman, the Countess Teresa Guicioli, which was to last until Byron left for Greece in 1823. Living in Ravenna and then Pisa, Byron published the verse drama, *Cain* (1821), followed a year later by the satirical poem, *A Vision of Judgement*.

Byron had become interested in the Greek war of independence from Turkey, which had begun in 1821, and in 1823 he sailed to Greece to support the cause. He was greeted warmly by the Greeks, and in

1824 he spent time and money organizing the Greek forces. But he became ill after going riding in drenching rain, and weakened by his doctors' insistence on bleeding him, he died of fever on April 19 in Missolonghi, at the age of thirty-six. He was mourned in Greece as a national hero.

Stanza CLXXVIII

In this stanza the poet expresses his deep appreciation of nature. He enjoys being in nature, whether it is in the woods or by the shore of the ocean. Even when he is alone by the sea, he finds a sense of connection, even though no people are there. He likes to listen to the sound of the waves. In line 5 he explains that his love of nature does not diminish his love of man. But in nature he is able to escape from himself and just become part of the universe. This gives rise to deep feelings inside him, so deep that he cannot express them, but neither can he hide them.

Stanza CLXXIX

The poet addresses the ocean directly and pays tribute to its power. On the earth, man has power and can destroy things. But his power ceases when he takes his ships on the ocean. He is at the mercy of the power of the ocean, as the thousands of wrecked ships on the ocean floor demonstrate. Man and his ships sink into the depths of the ocean, where the men have neither grave nor coffin, and where they lie is unknown.

Stanza CLXXX

This stanza continues the contrast between the power man wields on earth and his helplessness at sea. Man cannot despoil the ocean as he does the land. The ocean has contempt for the power man has on earth. The ocean can create a storm that tosses man up and down, causing him to pray for salvation, hoping that he can reach a port or other safe haven somewhere. But then the sea casts him down again and he is lost.

Stanza CLXXXI

This stanza further exposes the vanity of man's power in contrast to that of the sea. The first three lines refer to the bombardment of cities by ships during wartime. The walls of the cities do not protect them from attack, and the attacks destabilize nations and make kings fear for their lives. In line 4, the reference to "oak leviathans" is to the warships. Leviathan is a sea monster in the Bible, mentioned in Job, Isaiah, and the Psalms. The poet says that the warships are huge, but they mislead men into calling themselves lords of the sea, able to win battles through sea-power. But men forget that they are mortal (the reference to "clay" in line 5 is a reference to their mortality), so their claims to power are foolish. As the speaker points out in line 7, these great warships are treated as toys by the ocean, which destroys them and makes a mockery of their strength. The reference to the Armada is to the Spanish Armada that tried to invade England in 1588. Trafalgar refers to the naval battle between England and France in 1805. Both the Spanish

Armada and the French navy suffered much damage through storms before they could begin the battle. In fact, the Spanish Armada was almost completely destroyed and was never able to land in England.

Stanza CLXXXII

The poet contrasts the changing empires that men create with the constancy of the sea. He mentions the empires of Assyria, Greece, Rome, and Carthage. They have been destroyed many times over, by encroachments from the sea as well as by tyrants. All that is left that are "the stranger, slave, or savage"; the civilization has been destroyed. Deserts exist now where formerly there were flourishing human societies. But this does not apply to the sea, which is unchangeable except for the movement of the waves. It is unaffected by the passage of time. It is the same now as it was on the day of creation.

Stanza CLXXXIII

The speaker refers to the ocean as a mirror in which the power of God may be seen in storms. Whatever condition the sea is in, its vastness is a reflection of eternity. This is true whether the ocean is calm or rough, and wherever the ocean is found, whether at the poles of the earth, where it supplies ice, or in the tropical regions. The ocean is also generative; its slime produces all the creatures that populate its depths. Everything in the ocean obeys its laws, and the ocean always continues in its fathomless depths.

Stanza CLXXXIV

The poet confesses to the ocean that he has always loved it. He remembers the joy he felt when he was young and swam in the ocean and was carried along by it. He would play in the breaking waves, which were a delight to him. If the wind increased and the waves became frightening, he was not discouraged. He even enjoyed the fear that such events produced. In line 7 he explains this love of the ocean that he has always had. It was as if he was a child of the ocean and he trusted it wherever he was and in whatever circumstances. He put his hand on the "mane" of the ocean as if he were riding a favorite horse. Now he puts his hand again on the ocean, through the medium of the words he is writing in praise of it.

MEDIA ADAPTATIONS

- *The Romantic Poets*, a ten-disc set of CDs released by HighBridge Audio (2005) includes excerpts from *Childe Harold's Pilgrimage*.

- *The Poetry of Lord Byron* is an audiobook released by HarperCollins Audiobook on audio cassette in 1997.

- *Poems by Lord Byron* is available from http://www.audible.com as an audio download from Saland Publishing.

THEMES

Union with Nature

The first stanza of this excerpt from *Childe Harold's Pilgrimage* expresses the theme of love of nature and union with nature. When the poet is alone in nature, whether in the woods or by the sea, he feels "pleasure" and "rapture." He feels a sense of communion with nature's presence, which is why he is not lonely even when in solitary places. He does not miss human company when in the company of nature. Perhaps most importantly, in nature he is able to get beyond himself, so to speak, to leave behind "all I may be, or have been before" and become absorbed in the universe. His human identity as a particular man in a particular place, with all the usual petty human day-to-day concerns and thoughts of the past, seems to melt away in the presence of nature. He becomes a larger being, no longer plagued by the usual small sense of self, of "I" but simply a calm, untroubled part of the wider whole. This feeling he acquires in the presence of nature is ineffable, that is, it cannot be expressed in words, as the speaker admits in the final line. The theme of love of nature returns in the final stanza, when the speaker recalls the delight he felt when as a child he would swim in the ocean. He was like a child trusting a parent; even the turbulence of the waves did not disturb his feeling that the ocean was a benevolent thing, something he could play in and enjoy.

Eternity and Time

Whereas the first stanza in this excerpt describes a kind of union with nature, the remaining stanzas suggest the opposite: The ocean is set apart from man and has the capacity to destroy him. The ocean is eternal, but man and his works are transient. They come and go. The ocean is presented as an adversary of man. Man thinks he can tame it, building ships that sail the ocean and using them as powerful means of waging war, but the ships are flimsy and weak when compared to the power of the sea. They can be destroyed in a moment, and all man's prayers make no difference to his fate. The ocean mocks his arrogance.

Man's proper place is on the earth, where he has his power, even though, as the poem states, he uses it too often for destructive purposes. At sea, the tables are turned. As the second line of stanza CLXXIX states, "Ten thousand fleets sweep over thee in vain." Man's power, when it comes to the sea, is an illusion. He is always at the mercy of the ocean. And unlike the earth, which always carries the scars of man's destructive impulses, the ocean swallows up man and his ships and leaves no trace on its smooth surface. The ocean always remains what it is, "boundless, endless, and sublime" (stanza CLXXXIII).

The speaker uses this eternal nature of the ocean to set up a contrast between eternity and time.

The ocean is "the image of Eternity" (stanza CLXXXIII), but man belongs to the temporal realm. His is the sphere of history, the record of man's doings on the earth, in which things that once were are no more. The poet cites history several times, both in general and specific terms. He mentions the Spanish Armada and the battle of Trafalgar, as well as the ancient empires of Assyria, Greece, Rome, and Carthage. Powerful in their day, these empires are now described only in the pages of history books. Yet the ocean still laps the same shores, exactly as it did during the heyday of those empires. As stanza CLXXXII states, "Time writes no wrinkle on thine azure brow."

TOPICS FOR FURTHER STUDY

- Write a short poem about the ocean, a lake, or water generally. How does being around water make you feel?

- Make a drawing or painting of the sea, with a human observer. What qualities will you try to convey in this picture?

- Using PowerPoint or similar program, give a class presentation in which you describe, with slides and a map, Byron'sGrand Tour of 1809-11 and his later travels to Venice and Rome.

- Consult *George Gordon, Lord Byron* (Oxford University Press, 2001), by Martin Garrett. This is a biography written for young adults. Pay particular attention to the sections that cover Byron's writing of *Childe Harold's Pilgrimage*. Write an essay in which you describe Byron's travels in Europe, why he decided to write the poem, and what its main characteristics are.

It is through this contrast between eternity and time that the poet exposes the smallness of man's life when set against the largeness of the ocean. Man has his hopes, feelings, and desires, but the ocean is impersonal. It knows nothing and cares nothing for such things. It will continue unchanged long after generations of men have come and gone. The poem thus uses the image of the ocean to give a vision of the vast stretch of time and the changeable, transient nature of human life when set against eternity. Time rushes on, but eternity always remains what it is.

Spenserian Stanza

These stanzas are written in what is called Spenserian stanzas. The Spenserian stanza is named after Elizabethan English poet Edmund Spenser (1552-1599), who invented the form in his poem *The Faerie Queene*. The Spenserian stanza consists of nine lines. The first eight lines are written in iambic pentameter and the last line in iambic hexameter (also known as an Alexandrine).

An iamb is a poetic foot in which an unstressed syllable is followed by a stressed syllable. (A foot consists of two or three syllables, either one strongly stressed syllable and one lightly stressed syllable or one strong stress and two lighter ones.) A pentameter consists of five feet. An iambic hexameter consists of six iambic feet.

The poet occasionally varies the meter. The most common variation is the substitution of a trochee for an iamb at the beginning of the line, in the first foot. A trochee consists of a stressed syllable followed by an unstressed one; it is therefore the opposite of an iamb. The inversion of the first foot occurs, for example, in line 4 of stanza CLXXIX, in which the first syllable, "Stops," is stressed. The inversion makes the word stand out against the expected regular metrical base. Similar inversions to create a trochaic first foot occur in stanza CLXXX ("Spurning"), stanza CLXXXIII ("Glasses" and "Icing"), stanza CLXXXIV ("Borne"), and elsewhere.

Occasionally the line contains an extra unstressed syllable, as in the last line of stanza CLXXXI: "Alike the Armada's pride, or spoils of Trafalgar." This is known as a feminine ending. In a regular iambic line, the final syllable is stressed, and such lines are called masculine endings.

The rhyme scheme is as follows: line 1 rhymes with lines 3; line 2 rhymes with lines 4, 5, and 7; line 6 rhymes with lines 8 and 9. The rhyme scheme can be described as *a b a b b c b c c*.

The Spenserian stanza was used by other English Romantic poets, including John Keats, Percy Bysshe Shelley, and William Wordsworth.

Apostrophe

An apostrophe is a figure of speech in which a poet directly addresses an absent person, inanimate object, or abstract quality. In this case, six of the seven stanzas consist of apostrophes to the ocean, beginning with stanza CLXXIX, "Roll on, thou deep and dark blue Ocean—roll!" The poet addresses the ocean using the terms "thou" and "thy" throughout. These are archaic words used for the most part only in reference to God. The poet's use of them shows the reverence with which he regards the ocean, and the god-like status he ascribes to it. He writes as if he were approaching a powerful, conscious being.

The Romantic Movement

The romantic movement in English literature is usually dated from 1798 to 1832. The principal poets associated with the movement are William Wordsworth (1770-1850), Samuel Taylor Coleridge (1772-1834), and William Blake (1757-1827), who were the first generation of Romantics, and Percy Bysshe Shelley (1792-1822), John Keats (1795-1821), and Lord Byron, the second generation.

Although Blake was publishing his poems himself in the 1790s, he did not have an audience, so it was the publication of Wordsworth and Coleridge's *Lyrical Ballads* in 1798 that really marked the beginning of the romantic movement. Wordsworth brought a new language to poetry, replacing the formal poetic diction of the eighteenth century with a simpler language that captured the way ordinary people—the country folk, not the educated middle classes—actually spoke. Wordsworth also emphasized the role of feeling, famously defining poetry in his Preface to *Lyrical Ballads* as the "spontaneous overflow of powerful feelings." Following Wordsworth, the Romantic poets did not just describe objectively what they were perceiving; they also recorded their own reactions to it, often in terms of their feelings as much as their thoughts.

COMPARE & CONTRAST

- **Early 1800s:** Aristocratic young men mainly from England undertake the Grand Tour of Europe to broaden their education and become more cultivated. Travel takes a long time and can only be undertaken by those with adequate financial means. In the 1840s, however, the development of mass transit by rail, as well as steamships, enables more people to tour Europe.

  Today: Cheap air and train travel, as well as efficient roads, make it easy for anyone with a modest amount of money to explore Europe.

- **Early 1800s:** The romantic movement flourishes in England and Germany. In Germany, the leading literary figures are Johann Wolfgang von Goethe, Novalis, Achim von Armin, E. T. A. Hoffman, and Heinrich Heine.

  Today: The dominant cultural movement in literature and the arts is postmodernism. In poetry, free verse is the most popular form, but many poets also write in traditional form and meter.

- **Early 1800s:** When the poets Byron and Shelley are in Italy, the country is a collection of republics (Venice, Genoa), duchies (Milan, Parma, Modena, Tuscany), a monarchy (Naples), and theocracy (the Papal States), all under the domination of Austria. The movement toward Italian independence and unification gathers force.

Today: Italy is an independent republic. It is a parliamentary democracy and a member of the European Community and the North Atlantic Treaty Organization (NATO).

Wordsworth and Coleridge are associated with the Lake District in northwest England, which provided Wordsworth in particular with almost endless inspiration for poetry. A deep appreciation of nature is a characteristic of Romantic poetry in general, often expressed through a lyric poem, which is a short poem in which a speaker describes his state of mind or feelings. The Romantic lyric poem often uses nature as a point of departure. The speaker may present his often troubled feelings as he contemplates a natural scene. Then after a process in which his mind and heart interact with nature, the poem rounds back where it began, and the speaker feels more tranquil, having resolved some difficult emotion or gained new insight into a problem. Examples of this form, often known as the "conversation poem" because of the informal language used, include Coleridge's "The Eolian Harp" and "Frost at Midnight." Keats and Shelley varied the form, often apostrophizing the object of their contemplation, as Byron did in the apostrophe to the ocean from *Childe Harold's Pilgrimage*. Examples include Shelley's "To a Sky-Lark" and "Ode to the West Wind," and Keats's "Ode to a Nightingale."

The Romantics valued imagination over reason. They believed that the imagination provided access to a higher level of truth and a clearer, more holistic way of seeing things than the rational intellect. They were explorers in the sphere of human consciousness who wanted to expand their realm of experience. Romantics, therefore, took an interest in the supernatural (Coleridge's "Christabel," for example), as well as in dreams (Keats's "The Eve of St. Agnes"). In general, they believed that the poet was a prophet, a man who could see further and understand more deeply than the ordinary person, and whose voice should be respected. Shelley, Wordsworth, and Blake certainly held such views, although Byron did not.

The Romantic period was a time of revolution in France followed by the Napoleonic wars throughout much of Europe. Wordsworth and Blake were at first enthusiastic supporters of the French Revolution, believing in its ideals of freedom and equality. Later, however, when the revolution betrayed its ideals and France set out on wars of conquest, they turned against it. Wordsworth became politically conservative in his later years, although Blake remained a radical, opposing all forms of war and empire. Of the second generation of Romantics, both Shelley and Byron aligned themselves with the cause of liberty. Byron was sympathetic to the growing movement toward Italian reunification and freedom from Austrian rule. He also supported the Greeks in their war of independence, a cause for which he gave his life.

On the domestic front, Blake and Shelley were particularly aware of the social problems caused by the Industrial Revolution. There had been a shift in population from rural areas to the cities where the new factories were, but factory workers toiled for long hours in difficult and often dangerous conditions. Social unrest grew, reaching a peak in the 1810s, and culminating in the Peterloo massacre in Manchester in August 1819. Sixty thousand workers had gathered at a public meeting to demand political reform. They were attacked by mounted militiamen, and eleven unarmed citizens were killed, with many more being injured. Shelley was indignant about the massacre and thought that England was on the brink of a revolution that would pit the oppressors against the oppressed. Byron learned of the incident in Italy, and he too thought England was facing imminent revolution. However, the revolution did not occur, and political reform had to wait until the passing of the Great Reform Act in 1832.

CRITICAL OVERVIEW

These seven stanzas from Canto IV of *Childe Harold's Pilgrimage* have always been held in high regard. Many editions of Byron's works that present only sections of *Childe Harold's Pilgrimage* are likely to include them, and they are also included in numerous anthologies. Many critics over the last fifty years of the twentieth century commented on these stanzas. M. K. Joseph, in *Byron, the Poet*, points out that the "concluding seascape" in Canto IV, as well as other elements in the Canto, such as the "river-poem" and the "mountain-poem" draws on "the whole repertory of forms provided by eighteenth-century topographical poetry." Byron is able to give this convention "renewed life by working from first-hand material and the resources of a receptive imagination." In *Childe Harold's Pilgrimage, Cantos III and IV and The Vision of Judgement*, Patricia M. Ball notes how in the stanzas immediately preceding the apostrophe to the ocean, Byron makes other references to the sea "until he is ready to unleash the full assault and bring the idea of the sea to us in its most exalted and awesome form." In the apostrophe itself he "emphas[es] the vastness of his subject by repeated superlatives and a vocabulary of power and grandeur." Peter J. Manning in *Byron and His Fictions* draws attention to how the apostrophe ends rather differently than it had begun. He writes: "Byron strives to conclude *Childe Harold IV* with a peroration of definitive and comprehensive closure. His grandly rhetorical address to the Ocean nonetheless gradually modulates into nostalgic childhood memories." Manning also points out that the apostrophe begins with the ocean as "an epitome of masculine power" but ends with an image of the ocean as a "docilely feminine creature supporting the young Byron." Andrew Rutherford, in *Byron: A Critical Study*, views the apostrophe to the ocean in light of Canto IV as a whole. The canto is "a long meditation on Time's works, defeats, and victories, culminating in the address to Ocean, which for Byron is a symbol of Eternity."

SOURCES

Ball, Patricia M., *Childe Harold's Pilgrimage, Cantos III and IV and The Vision of Judgement*, Basil Blackwell, 1968, p. 58.

Lord Byron, *Childe Harold's Pilgrimage*, Canto III, stanza LXXII, Canto IV, stanzas CXXVIII-CXXX, CLXXVIII-CLXXXIV, in *Lord Byron: Selected Poems*, edited with a preface by Susan J. Wolfson and Peter J. Manning, Penguin, 1996, pp. 440, 552, 567-69.

Central Intelligence Agency, *The World Factbook: Italy*, https://www.cia.gov/library/publications/the-worldfactbook/geos/it.html (accessed September 27, 2009).

Grant, A. J., and Harold Temperley, *Europe in the Nineteenth and Twentieth Centuries (1789-1950)*, 6th ed., Longmans, 1969.

Joseph, M. K., *Byron, the Poet*, Victor Gollancz, 1966, pp. 75-76.

Manning, Peter J., *Byron and His Fictions*, Columbia University Press, 1966, pp. 96-97.

Marchand Leslie, A., ed., *Lord Byron: Selected Letters and Journals*, Belknap Press of Harvard University Press, 1982.

Rutherford, Andrew, *Byron: A Critical Study*, Oliver and Boyd, 1961, p. 97.

Shelley, Percy Bysshe, "Ozymandias," in *Shelley's*

Poetry and Prose, selected and edited by Donald H. Reiman and Sharon B. Powers, Norton, 1977, p. 103.

Woodward, Christopher, *In Ruins*, Pantheon Books, 2001, p. 13.

Wordsworth, William, *Lyrical Ballads: Wordsworth and Coleridge*, edited with introduction, notes and appendices by R. L. Brett and A. R. Jones, Methuen, 1968, p. 266.

FURTHER READING

Abrams, M. H., *Natural Supernaturalism: Tradition and Revolution in Romantic Literature*, Norton, 1971.

> This renowned study of Romanticism examines poetry and philosophy in England and Germany, showing how Romantic writers shared certain themes and styles. Although Byron is not the focus of the book, it does provide valuable context for understanding the literary movement in which Byron placed himself.

Berry, Francis, "The Poet of *Childe Harold*," in *Byron: A Symposium*, edited by John Jump, Harper & Row, 1975, pp. 35-51.

> In this essay, Berry argues that T. S. Eliot's negative assessment of Byron, made in the 1930s and quite influential, no longer applies.

Grosskurth, Phyllis, *Byron: The Flawed Angel*, Houghton Mifflin, 1997.

> This is a lively, well-written psychoanalytic biography that delves into Byron's inner life. It is free of jargon and provides some valuable insights into this most fascinating of

literary giants. Grosskurth gained access to the Lovelace papers, which previous biographers had been denied, and the information contained therein enables her to trace in detail the collapse of Byron's marriage.

Marchand, Leslie, *Byron's Poetry: A Critical Introduction*, Houghton Mifflin, 1965, pp. 36-59.

Marchand is one of the leading twentieth-century scholars of Byron, and in this introductory chapter on *Childe Harold's Pilgrimage*, he argues that it is the finest confessional poem in English Romanticism; Byron speaks with a universal voice, expressing thoughts common to all men.